Afterbirth

ACKNOWLEDGMENTS

Many thanks to the journals where these poems found homes in their
early stages, including *Bloodroot Literary Magazine*, where "Buttercup" first
appeared.

Publisher: Leah Huete de Maines
Editor: Christen Kincaid
Cover Art: Stella Rodenberg
Author Photo: Joshua Lucca
Cover Design: Elizabeth Maines McCleavy

Order online: www.finishinglinepress.com
        also available on amazon.com

Author inquiries and mail orders:
Finishing Line Press
PO Box 1626
Georgetown, Kentucky 40324
USA

Contents

How long can I be a wall, keeping the wind off?
Sylvia Plath

The Mothers

gather in corners, eggs perforating
    their torsos.

I slip gloves on, knock my boot
    against the bed. A kindness.

They are large, fatter than you
    might think, like a monkey's hand,

furred, crumpling in mine. Until I wrest

a rogue bull thistle from the loam
    in this darling husband-hammered

box, dislodging a soil-clot of roots
    with a jiggle, spidery black placenta,

they are invisible. Blooming like mushrooms
    in some wet time lapse,

these burgeoning clumps of clay
    bare their teeth, turning

to the clumsy shadow blocking
    the sun. Delicate as wolves,

they amble over chasms. I expect them,
    and still some force lifts

me, always, from my knees, dirt-dusted
    hairs pricking my neck like the promise

of lightning. On their backs,
    countless little selves

ripple and teem, shifting like sand.

Motherhood as Abstraction

I guess I craved the heft, a warp and weft of scars,

proximity to otherside, thinning of a veil.

Longed to press my face against a thin pane of glass.

Loved my finite grasp of endlessness.

Had much to give before I gave.

Wished some force would drain me, pour out my spoiled self.

I sipped Southern Comfort from a McDonald's cup,

Stumbled through morning shifts just fine.

I had more time than I knew, so I slept.

Before lifting a steaming baby from my body, I loved the ghost child I summoned with incense and night visions.

I was heedless and chaos-drunk.

Believed—foolish—I would do right.

Birth Work

Skin fuzz thins and sinks
through ribs, fine as smelt.

I'm eight. I peel a dense sheet of moss
under the crabapple, flicking long-legged spides,

tuck my fur children into their bed.
Maybe next time: tender mewling,

a tiny heartbeat lifted into the air,
a delicate knock against my palm,

and the smell of birth, tangling
in my hands like yarn.

Crystal River

One morning in January,
I appear to my father.

Get in, he says. A goliath bull slides
from the dark river beneath us,

his back marked by rudders and blades,
tinged green by algae. My brother

refuses, sits.My father pries my fingers
from the edge of the boat.

I close my eyes, slip into the murk.
At the surface, the chill forms

a bitter film. Underwater, I can see the bottom,
closer than I thought; the cows and their calves

grazing, lazy. Flickers of small fish
punctuate my sunken view.

I follow the manatee, a dull male moon
sweeping the sunless question of the river.

My mouth opens. Silt settles
on my tongue.

Beauty Hill

We're lost, I say, *dogs too,*
and a silence rises in the pines

like an alarm, sky dimpling
with a threat of an evening snow.

Sinkholes pockmark these woods,
swallowing our dogs for a day,

maybe two, before spitting them
out, bashful and crusty with earth.

We look for our own tracks
in the snow, any proof of ourselves.

We puzzle over a new ravine.
A boy in Epsom had just been found

two miles from his home, frozen
to the ground like a stone.

I put my hands on your face
and say, again, *we are going to die.*

I loved being bearer of bad news.
Still do. You knew better.

How do you do it? How
do you always find the way?

The Lab

My father keeps his specimens
in tanks and jars and bins.
The scent of aldehyde meets us
at the door. Under the glare
of fluorescent light, burnished millipedes
tuck their tails into harmless coils.
A wax-yellow plastic-wrapped piglet
curls in a minifridge, surrounded
by stacks of frogs chilling in plastic sacks.
I lift the arthropods to my arms
and feel legion legs licking closer,
inch by inch, to my heart.
Peel open the graying hairless cat,
a *female*, he tells me, taking inventory
of her dumb contents and replacing them,
piece by piece, until she is whole.
I finger the antiseptic sheep's eye,
sickly blue iris lolling on a silver tray,
roll it over my tongue like a jawbreaker,
pinch the eye between thumb and forefinger,
scalpel in hand. To slice open the slick globe,
draining its golden visions into my palm.

Buttercup

splayed out by some secret poison
in the center of the barn,
her breath snapping like a flag,
a flame. I peered through the window
sparrows mistook for a portal,
dropping like the green-hulled walnuts
that stained my fingers orange, careful
of the glass. She couldn't stand.
We didn't own a gun so we called
the neighbors. Stupid chambers
of her stupid belly blocked by plastic.
Why do I remember winter
when I know it was summer?
The blanket crisping over a space heater,
almost catching. My mother's arms
over me. And a sound like the lake
breaking open in the dusk.
Summer, I draped myself over her back
in the sun like a hide, curing. She, the color
and comfort of peanut butter.
My stepfather knelt in the wet hay,
emptying her stomachs with care.
We inefficient farmers
kept countless mooncalves.
They gathered at the front door.
I wanted to love them.
I really did.

A Dog Loses an Eye

her head   hung low   in the middle

       of the dead   -end road   the hillside

peppered   with narrow homes   an eye

      monument   to an eye   long gone

a puncture   swollen shut   like a mountain

      punched   empty   I didn't stay long

only saw her   like that once   or

     twice   before I left   I didn't belong

but my grandmother   begged me   to stay

     that summer   we watched *Breaking Bad*

6 hours a day   and I taunted her

     to go   *outside*   take a walk

in sunlight   seething   at the soft hump

    of her   back   wishing her

tougher crueler   wishing wishing might

    protect   some precious   brutality

or   my mother   or me

    wishing   one of us   stronger

wishing   dollars   wishing

     silence   bottle green   birdsong

morning   on the porch   and her ugly

     dog   sally   eyes bright

the bitterness   of folgers   warming

     our hands   yes

that day   her hands   raking

     my hair   ghostflesh   waking

my arms   those gentle   scratches

     i kept   them   forever

wishing   we might   outlive

     the rage   lifting   our

hair   like   wind

Medjebama

In 1985, Mostar-Duvno's bishop Pavao Zanic determined that the
apparitions were not authentic, i.e., not of supernatural origin.

1.   Visions
Visions whisper to impressionable girls
whisper to impressionable girls whisper
to impressionable girls whisper to

until they settle here in Alabama
god only knows why and I'm thinking
of the longleaf pine striking the fading sky
from the center of an uneven field
like a snake and the seething crowd
sewn up by a hem of stacked stones

2.   Martha
even after you scolded me
for revealing my collarbones
I followed you to the place
you believed would change everything
the home on the edge
of the property reeked
of baby powder and doilies
a life-sized doll house
where women like yourself
plinked coins into jars that populated
every surface like mushrooms fruiting
the air was starchy and pale
somebody painted a room with blood
and I froze in the doorway
but when the buses spilled their contents
into the field and four thousand
people fell to their knees
and stared at the sun as it sank
into a web of trees you looked
at me and knowing what was best
but not knowing why I got on my knees
and I stayed there for a very long time

Partus

to bear

when my grandmother dies   my mother says

         I can hardly   *bear it*

partus: bring/bringing forth   like
    it brings up a lot for me

to bare oneself: splitting a body open

a body scored like an apple

fingernails digging   into the stem end of

wedging   under taut skin

juice stinging the quick lobes split   in half

with a crack and twist   also: young

green leaflet   unfurling   dreamlet internally

curling pink   pea green seed embedded

under seawater muscle fascia fat skin

four years after her mother   dies   my mother

says   *I can hardly*   *bear it*

before she died I curled up   next to her in bed

asked   *can you feel him?*

no   and she didn't   look at me

two months later   my son burst   into the new year

I bore him   he wore me   like a yoke

dove   into the florid light   of January

fell   into   an empty space

I can

          hardly

Coffin Birth

At first the remains look random,
scattered by gravity

like broken branches in the yard.
A female bulge softens

and swells to expel
a loose-limbed mini corpse.

In death, even, the body yearns
to empty.

The belly gathers gases
and bloats,

inhale and exhale
powered by rot.

Afterbirth

1.
from the corner of my bedroom
I watch my otherself
will that stubborn disc of blood
submarine hatch screwed tight
a prayer I held so close
nobody could hear me
every moment brings me closer
to seeing her face
now it plays in reverse
every moment pulls me further
from her strawberry moon face
and I pull at the cord limp and green
that once tied us and watch
my belly swelling with blood
dip where the thick organ
latches like an octopus
bloodroots tendriling
where our blood once communed
but never mixed and I know
now I could not detach
to save my life I could not let go
even after she was clipped
from me my body clung
to what she left behind
but in the dream room
there is only a great soft work
so I reach down feel the small bones
in her tiny wrist this fresh limb
reaching out of myself and I hold her
hand I say *come out come out*
I say *I am ready*
for you now

Ghost Belly

In the days just post- her belly quivers and dips when she laughs, soft-sac of empty, bag of fluid swelling to fill the space left by the child. Her breast inflates until the nipple recedes into the roundswell. Baby can't find a latch, so clamps. Blood pinpricks and pulls to just beneath the surface of tender skin, a first child-made bruise. A quickening: intestines settle into their restful right positions, but feels like something else, like the swipe of a ghost hand, a pea-sized toe gliding across the underbelly of her belly. The child is crying, yes, gulping air in the bassinet at eye level. There is no other, she knows, but the body lies. Sleep sifts down and out when she stands for the 50th time. Her waist spills like an open sack of flour, nausea grinds at the edges like sand.

Powerball

That my eyes are always hot and wet and strange from smiling.

That I always seem to laugh at the wrong moment.

That we don't go to church, but I buy a Powerball ticket every
Sunday.

That I become one with my couch until my husband pries my
phone out of my hand with his teeth.

That I spend days prying stubborn ditch lilies from the red clay
dirt I've been cursed with. (We could eat the bulbs if
we needed to, I think, and feel a stab of guilt for tossing
them to the hens.)

That this June is unusually cool.

That the garden is floundering.

That you've never waded through snow. Might not ever.

That the trash is overflowing. One can see it from the road.

That the bees are gone and the hummingbirds visit only once in
a blue moon and the tree of paradise leaves a ghost
rot on our skin when we brush against it.

That the white sun hurts your eyes.

That a street dissects our yard and so you cannot play alone.

That the only creatures who will survive this are spindly & sting.

That I have to leave you in the yard to move the laundry, so I
     count as you creep to the slick black road. One, two,
     three. Is a car coming? You could be halfway there by
     now. I pray you go slow, and run to the window.
     One of you is digging a hole, the other raises a fist to the
     sky.

Afterbirth II

My daughter must be
memory keeper.

Mine is gone.
From those arch

spring days, I only hold
sensations flattened

by the distance of time:
nails pressing crescents

into my sick, damp palms.
My wrist cramped, jaw

wound tight in those mad
morning hours.

She asks me now and always,
what is that?

It sounds like petals dribbling
from the tulip poplar;

like bees—no, wasps, hurrying
from one crushed bloom

to another; a blessing,
questioning, like a blossom

falling from her mouth.

King Tide

You can't just go around abusing people,
I say and he says *I'm calling the police*

I'm holding my son to my breast
at the Circle K and maybe

that was my mistake, parading
the softness of my life

and I can't tell if he'll get back in his car
or slice us open with some hidden blade.

Missouri night pours over my back—
king tide of heat, dampened by shade.

They're always veterans, these men
who could be my grandfather,

who pull up in their sedans,
medicinal smoke billowing,

hands trembling, voices harsh and cruel.
This cruelty familiar as a song

haunting us from every radio station.
These are the death throes, we laugh,

our sloped shoulders touching, and always
with my sisters/mother/children in tow,

I am reminded of what it means to be
at their mercy.

Always at their god
awful mercy.

Whaleheart
for Asa

Salt slaps our cheeks & we narrow
our eyes to better see the promise
of colossal bodies blackening
the horizon. I've wished for this
forever, or since you were four
and still wresting words every day
with the un-help of your mulish tongue,
piercing voice occluding your throat
like a clot. How hard those days were.
How toilsome that unbudging tongue,
even as you hurled your slight body
against it like a locked door.

Your comfort at this age:
Secrets of the Whales at least seven
times every day, Sigourney's voice
perfect and smooth as the Atlantic.

When I was pregnant, I dreamed always
of whales. The first story I ever read to you
was Moby Dick (abridged).

Now, the catamaran bounces on choppy waves
as we pick up speed and you shout, I'm scared.
I know the perfect prayer and whisper it
into your ear. Your limbs soften, calm breath
pours over my shoulder as the water rocks us, gentle.

Sigourney never tells. Or, at least,
anything spoken aloud is no longer secret.
The *whales have culture*, she says.
K, k, k, you punctuate, which means
from the top so I start the program
from the beginning.

Truthfully, we've never been together
on a boat. You've inherited different family
traditions which mostly involve
sitting together on a couch that sags
like an overloaded life-raft. And the truth,
in this moment that calls from the other side
of the page, is that you are still learning
to speak, still grappling with the silent rage
of being misunderstood, your voice
still an invention of my fantasy.

You can use your whole body, you say.
I didn't know, I move.

On the boat in my dreams we are alone.
(It is captained by the wind.)
I call you to the edge, the railing—
what is that called? I could say
brink, verge, fringe, or brim—
and all would be right
and wrong. I help you clamber
up to see a humpback, barnacled
and black, surfacing from unfathomable depths,
belching acrid steam into our shared breath.
I can't stop saying that word:
together. The whale's breath is loud,
a percussive shush—blessing of spume—
and without effort—without extraordinary effort,
we both shout "oh!" together and my voice catches
on the terrible wonder in my throat.

With Thanks

Many thanks to my mentors at Bennington: April Bernard, Carmen Gimenez-Smith, and Mark Wunderlich, for handling my entry into the world of poetry, and my baby poems, with generous care.

Thank you to the folks at Sundress Academy for the Arts, for giving me ample space and time to submerge fully in the waters of these poems.

Thank you to my partner in all things, Josh, for believing, always, that my art matters (despite my best efforts to convince you otherwise).

Thank you to my children, for enriching my life in such a way that makes me actually want to live it, and, subsequently, to write about it.

Lastly, I must thank my mother, and the lineage of mothers who are the reason I am here, writing this, today. Nothing would be possible without you.

Clara Strong lives in Indiana, where she now resides with her partner and their two children. Her poems have appeared in *Bloodroot Literary Magazine, Cutleaf,* and *Rascal,* and have been twice nominated for both a Pushcart Prize and Best New Poetry. She received her undergraduate degree from Antioch College in 2016 and her MFA from the Bennington Writing Seminars in 2020. She currently teaches Creative Writing at the University of Evansville. This is her first poetry collection.

www.ingramcontent.com/pod-product-compliance
Lightning Source LLC
Chambersburg PA
CBHW022103080426
42734CB00009B/1480